A Gift for

Sofia Noelle Zielinski

Given by

Hebron Preschool

This Day of

March 22, 2015

Sweet Dreams

A Companion Book of Bedtime Scriptures
Based on the *Sweet Dreams* CD
A *Lifetime Scripture Songs*™ Book
First Edition

By Cassie Byram
Illustrated by Brennen McElhaney

Scripture Translations:
Updated King James Version
The World English Bible

Published by Oodles World, LLC
Asheville, North Carolina

ISBN 978-0-9847760-1-6

www.CassieByram.com
www.OodlesWorld.com

Designed and created in USA

CPSIA Tracking Label Information
Printing: Coburn Printing Ink
Job Number: 12-1219
Date of Production: September 2012
Printed in Guangdong Province, China

Cassie Byram

SWEET DREAMS

Illustrated by Brennen McElhaney

LIFETIME SCRIPTURE SONGS™

for all God's children

★ SWEET

Meditate Upon These Things

Philippians 4:8-9

Whatever things are true,
Whatever things are noble,
Whatever things are just and pure,
Whatever things are lovely,
Think upon these things.

Think of all these things,
Think of all these things.
Meditate upon these things.

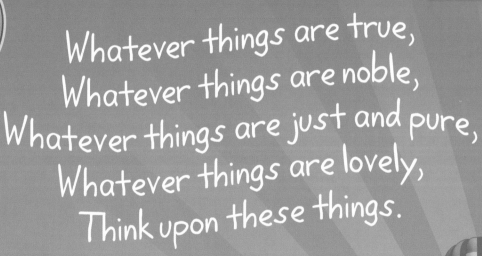

D R E A M S

Whatever is of good report,
If there is any virtue,
If anything is praise worthy,
Whatever things are lovely,
Think upon these things.

Think of all these things, think of all these things.
Meditate upon these things.

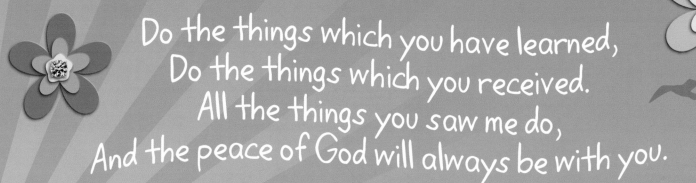

Do the things which you have learned,
Do the things which you received.
All the things you saw me do,
And the peace of God will always be with you.

Think of all these things, think of all these things.
Meditate upon these things.

Treasures in Heaven
Matthew 6:19-21

Do not lay up for yourselves
Treasures on earth, treasures on earth.
Do not lay up for yourselves
Treasures on earth, treasures on earth.

DREAMS

Where moth and rust destroy, where thieves break in.
But lay up for yourselves treasures in heaven.

For where your treasure is,
There your heart will be.
For where your treasure is,
There your heart will also be.

DREAMS

I will not fear what any man can do.
I will not fear. I will trust in You.

Whenever I feel I'm afraid,
I will trust in You.

Emmanuel!

Mighty God!

Counselor!

King of Kings!

I will trust in You.

God So Loved the World - John 3:16

For God so loved the world, He gave His only Son, that who believes in Him Should not perish but will have everlasting life.

DREAMS

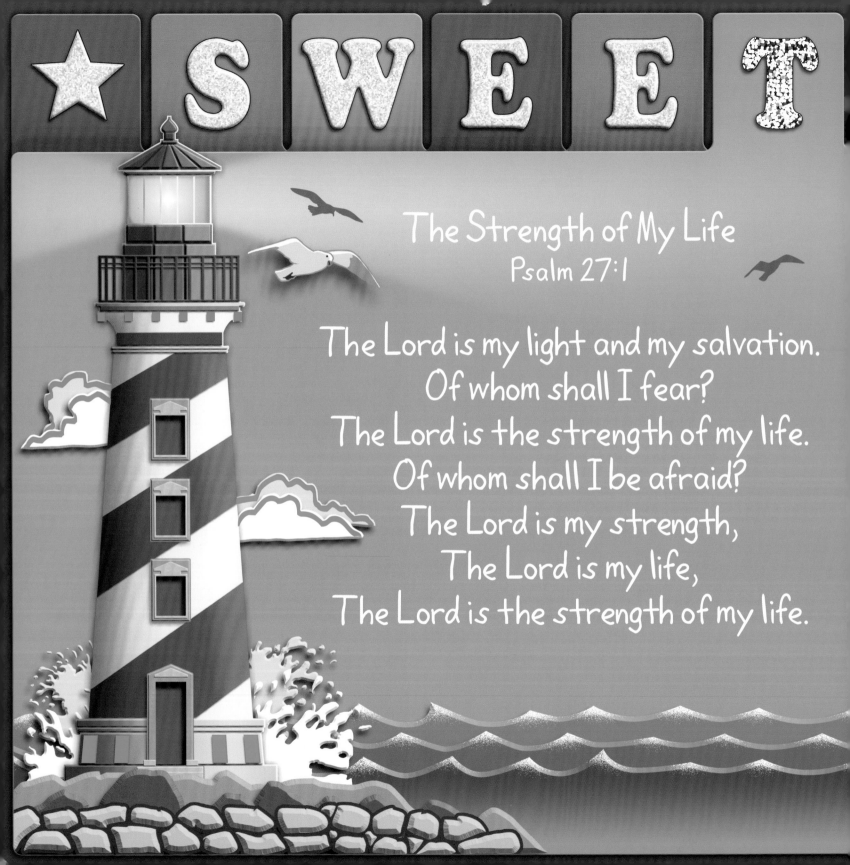

SWEET

The Strength of My Life
Psalm 27:1

The Lord is my light and my salvation.
Of whom shall I fear?
The Lord is the strength of my life.
Of whom shall I be afraid?
The Lord is my strength,
The Lord is my life,
The Lord is the strength of my life.

DREAMS

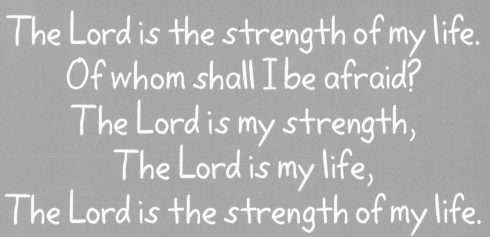

The Lord is the strength of my life.
Of whom shall I be afraid?
The Lord is my strength,
The Lord is my life,
The Lord is the strength of my life.

SWEET

Happy Are You
Proverbs 3:13-24

My child, by wisdom God made the earth.
By knowledge He founded the heavens.
With wisdom creation was given its birth.
Her paths are peaceful and pleasant.

Happy are you who find wisdom.
Don't let it depart from your eyes;
For she is better than silver and gold.
Happy are you who are wise.

HAPPY TRAILS!

DREAMS

When you lie down, you will not be afraid.
Your rest will be sweet as you sleep.
Then you shall walk safe as you go your way
When wisdom and knowledge you keep.

Happy are you who find wisdom.
Don't let it depart from your eyes;
For she is better than silver and gold.
Happy are you who are wise.
Happy are you who are wise.
Happy are you who are wise.

DREAMS

Walk in it, walk in it, and you will find rest for your souls.

For I am gentle and lowly in heart,
And you will find rest for your souls.
My yoke is easy, my burden is light,
And you will find rest for your souls.

Ask for the old paths where the way is good,
Stand in the way and see.
Ask for the old paths where the way is good,
And you will find rest for your souls.

★ SWEET

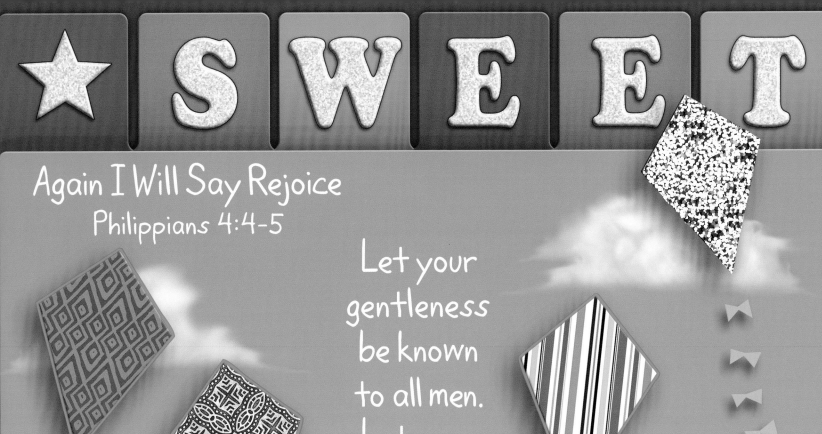

Again I Will Say Rejoice
Philippians 4:4-5

Let your gentleness be known to all men. Let your gentleness be known. The Lord is at hand.

Rejoice in the Lord always, Again I will say rejoice.

Rejoice in the Lord always, Again I will say rejoice.

DREAMS

Let your gentleness be known to all men. Let your gentleness be known. The Lord is at hand.

Rejoice in the Lord always, Again I will say rejoice.

Rejoice in the Lord always, Again I will say rejoice.

Again I will say

Rejoice

Rejoice

Rejoice

Rejoice

★ SWEET

He Who Keeps You
Psalm 121:3-8

He who keeps you will not slumber.
He who keeps you will not sleep.
Behold, He who keeps Israel shall neither slumber nor sleep.

He will lead me by day. He will keep me by night.
He will watch my going out. He will guide my coming in.

He who keeps you will not slumber.
He who keeps you will not sleep.
Behold, He who keeps Israel shall neither slumber nor sleep.

Behold, He who keeps Israel shall neither slumber nor sleep.

SWEET

A New Commandment
John 13:34-35

A new commandment I give to you
Love one another as I love you.

A new commandment I give to you
Love one another as I love you.

By this all will know
You are My disciples
If you have
Love.

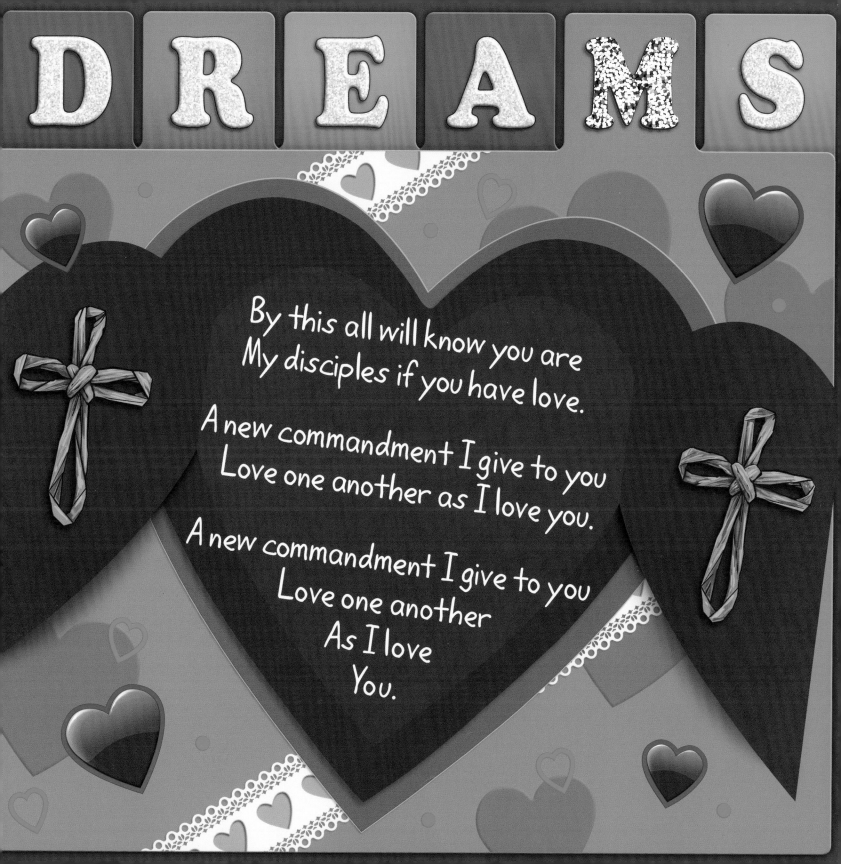

DREAMS

By this all will know you are
My disciples if you have love.

A new commandment I give to you
Love one another as I love you.

A new commandment I give to you
Love one another
As I love
You.

★ SWEET

He Shall Direct Your Path
Proverbs 3:5-6

Trust in the Lord with all your heart.
Don't lean on your own understanding.

In all your ways acknowledge Him and He shall direct,
He shall direct your path.

The *Sweet Dreams* book is part of the *Lifetime Scripture Songs*™ collection brought to you by Oodles World. Be sure to order the *Sweet Dreams* companion CD of original scripture-based lullabies. Just go to www.OodlesWorld.com to listen. Then add this beautiful resource to your music library for a blessing that will last a lifetime.

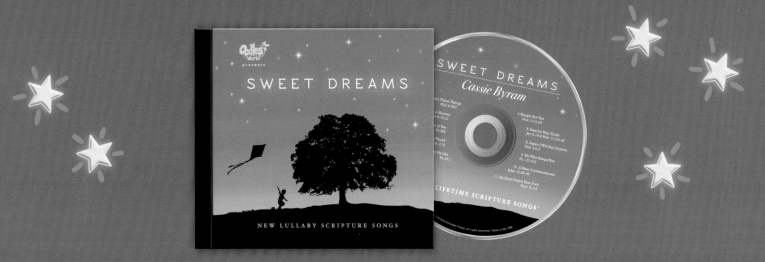

Oodles World provides trusted family entertainment, educational materials, and online connections and communities for families, churches, and non-profit organizations. An entire world of exciting new products is waiting for you at Oodles World!

Go to www.OodlesWorld.com to find out more...

AUTHOR

Cassie Byram is an award winning singer-songwriter whose voice has graced numerous recording projects for children and adults alike.

As a devoted wife and proud mother of two boys, Cassie understands the need for children to embrace God's Word at an early age. Her *Sweet Dreams* book along with the *Sweet Dreams* lullaby CD are wonderfully designed to not only soothe and comfort, but also to anchor the Word of God in the hearts of the youngest among us, at the earliest of ages. To find out more about Cassie, visit www.CassieByram.com.

ILLUSTRATOR

Brennen McElhaney serves as Creative Director for Oodles World. Classically trained at the Rhode Island School of Design, Brennen works with equal fluency creating both traditional and digital art. A signature member of the WNC *Plein Air* Painters, Brennen's fine art is represented in North Carolina by Gallery at Studio B, and Alta Vista Gallery. Brennen makes his home in Asheville, North Carolina with his wife and three children.